AREAS OF FOG

JOSEPH MASSEY

Areas of Fog

Shearsman Books
2009

Smaller as the days get I am beginning to write.
Someday no one will be able to read the world.
The line is an assemblage of broken smaller pieces.
The size of the world does not matter.
The end of the line is at the greatest juncture.
At that point where one may say Emergency
    and mean time.
The strong grasp that it has not yet begun to flow.
My words have always been written across vast distances.
I have often not known what was in my hand.
A poet needs the one who will tell him what
    he has done.
And especially the world which will tell him nothing.

—Clark Coolidge

First published in the United Kingdom by
Shearsman Books Ltd.,
58 Velwell Road,
Exeter EX4 4LD

www.shearsman.com

ISBN 978-1-84861-052-1

First Edition
Copyright © Joseph Massey, 2009

Cover image by Wendy Heldmann.
Copyright © Wendy Heldmann, 2007.

Design and Composition by Yuki Kites

TABLE OF CONTENTS

WITHIN HOURS

the day the held light
how it gets through

—Larry Eigner

Conversation

Horizon
bound by

road signs
and wires.

Low tide:
wide swaths

of mud
rub in.

Words, we
have none.

We're lost
in the tone

splayed
between

shadows
bending

with the
wind's pitch.

Pulse

Memory stifled
by the day's
lapse, the pursuant

pause infused with
skunk stench, traffic
rattle, a neighbor's
                    voice

strained to a
thin thump through

windows, walls.

Wait

Inside
a power line's

slack
center, the

afternoon
moon, half

full, is a
dent.

Listening to Joseph Ceravolo's Home Recordings

In the room
of a memory

of a room.
Static

brackets each
syllable.

Afternoon
effaces the floor

while the
pills take

effect.
All I will

amount to:
the hours

these walls
enclose

as song.

June

Dangled above
the traffic's rasp:

a contrail

a crow

a nail gun's echo.

Noon

Sun's thud
between
overhead
leaves
obscures
these bees
probing
a shadowed
plot's white
flowers
thumbed
out from
threshed
shrubs piled
beside a
sheet of
rusted metal.

August

In its lengthening
　　glare, dawn submerges
　　　　a dream's wreckage.

The mock orange
　　outside the window
　　　　flexes with weather.

Some semblance of quiet,
　　or near-quiet—
　　　　not quite silence, as if

silence ever is—drones.
　　A memory of a face
　　　　I remember forgetting,

how it sinks again
　　behind my head—
　　　　a shadow's palpable black.

Conditions

Haze, chalk dust
white, replaces
the space I

realize as
sky. Forests far
off, not too far,

on fire—so
goes the word
and this evidence.

Autumnal Equinox

Sober for once, for what—
for the words to budge.

We spent summer propped up
by each other's stuttering.

There *are* seasons here
if you squint. And there's

relief in the landscape's
sloughed off cusps of color

fallen over the familiar
landmarks, the familiar

trash—things that last.

Lost Coast

A cragged stack
in the gathering gray
surf, crowded by
seabirds,
their prehistoric
profiles. We
pull over
to argue, not
to talk,
but the words
won't form—
the terrain
overtakes them.
Bright litter
drifts into
sand and
small stones
at our feet.
Across the
street, cows
corral behind
barbed wire,
stock-still
in each other's
shadows. We
don't need words
to read the sun's

angle. We know
it will soon be
too dim
to navigate
the switchbacks
without guardrails
we descended
to arrive.

Impasse

Our senses
snag against

the world's burned,
blurred lists.

To bring it, the
radiant debris,

into coherence.
To collect

and recollect
what cannot be

apprehended,
only mended

again and again.
In that act

we're attached
to some kind of

ground—some clue
of an actual world—

never quite
beneath our feet.

Reading

for Devin Johnston

Looking out of
the window
for what won't
appear. And yet
there's a world
behind the glass,
within whose
insistence
we drift, forget.

BRAMBLE
a gathering of lunes

Let what is natural
say what it can...

—Robert Kelly

on the page, a stain
of an ant
            crushed in the margin

when you say it, say
it—what's there
            to be said—what's here

a snail's vacated
shell lies next
            to a wad of gum

late day, mosquitoes
drawn into
our conversation

television light
lies on the
American lawn

kitchen window fogged
where the moon
rises red & round

sun's still rewinding
into sky
the white morning haze

1860

Indian Island
where they sing
the world's renewal

2009

Indian Island
where a few
private docks reside

just the sound of them
engulfed in
      fog—shuffling southward

the weather's saying
what we won't
      say—what's between us

what's between us—this
chasm of
      vocabulary

a pigeon feather
flaps from a
           mound of pigeon shit

the intersection—
a glassed-in
           stream of talking hair

pretended to write
waited for
           her to walk past me

          pulp mill steam plume falls
up against
          dusk, the stretched red clouds

          there's a metaphor
here: the page
          behind the poem

          crows cackle over
an engine
          starting & stopping

in Cid's voice

you think there should be
more, but this
      this is all there is

remembering, as
a snail-streaked
      calla lily sways

remembering, as
the tarp whips
      against the fence post

remembering, as
rain slants in-
to my coffee cup

remembering, as
traffic takes
another long breath

through makeshift curtains
(blue blankets)
the sunset stutters

crescent moon cuts low
in cloudless
      black—scent of wet grass

weeds alight under
the window's
      television glow

moonlight a bat bats
above the
      shattered plum blossoms

three in the morning
a pigeon's
     trill threads through the wall

when the window throws
your image
     back, bound to the moon

there's a metaphor
behind each
     breath your life lets go

        dictation taken
daily from
        the weather's phrasing

        yellow-striped bumble-
bee bends slow-
        ly into sunlight

        dry-rotted, knotted
garden hose
        hidden within weeds

before we feel the
breeze we see
the weeds fold over

fire-hollowed house, the
lawn laden
with nameless blossoms

computer fan hums—
on your hands
the scent of cut grass

staring at water
in a glass
        you felt the earthquake

        rain gutter running
over with
        sun-stiffened weeds, leaves

        brick wall—six stories—
scaled by a
        pelican's shadow

last week's news: a pile
of rain-soaked
            pulp on the sidewalk

buds on a diseased
tree, at the
            edge of blossoming

here, the one speaking
& the one
            listening, is you

company tonight—
silence's
     cricket-warped surface

PROPERTY LINE

Here's the small
gasp

of this clearing...

—Rae Armantrout

Hill's red
tethered
edge—

berries
that numbed
your tongue.

■

Eucalyptus
limbs lisp

wind winds
off the bay.

Mosquitoes
dusk tugs
from the lawn

reflect against
the clenched
fuchsia buds.

■

Swallows
whisk the rifts

dusk dims
between leaves

on the tree
whose name

I refuse to find.

Torn through sequoia branches
the moon tears a path
        my fist follows to the door
anchored by a twelve pack.

■

Factory lights
crease night's
farthest seam

where hills
daub black
deeper than

the black en-
compassing.

Next
door's
flower's

scent
parts
the curtain.

■

Flies, sun-
dried, line
the windowsill.

Measure
what was summer.

Hummingbird
through a vortex of gnats
navigates nasturtiums

                        unraveled
        over a gravel path.

■

Honeysuckle
scent like
an open vowel

wrung out
in the rain's
gloss-

olalia.

Spider web
(wind-
ripped)

weighted with
a wet receipt.

■

Hills out-
lined

behind
haze

that
holds it

all in.

Hung on
to the weather's
edge

we read our-
selves
in place.

■

Glass
crushed

by a garbage
truck

cracks the
room's

silence in
half.

Fog torn
around
a crow

rowing
toward
a row of

eucalyptus.

■

Ourselves
in place—an edge
the weather's

wrought—some-
thing we read—
we hold—

we're the text of.

These interruptions

of color
in the overgrowth.

■

Wing-slur—

half a humming-

bird's body
swallowed by

one of the few
fuchsias left.

A gap
in the
black

clouds
where
the sun-

set clots.

■

This dusk-
colored
landscape

the rain

deepens

into night.

Power lines
dent the dawn.

What words I
woke with

dissolve.

■

After Bronk

Words
occur
to gather

a world—

not *the*

world.

Enough to make
the foliage
flinch,

wind slits.

Music sifts

out of a house.

Abandoned Lot

1.

Bees inscribe the fog
and funnel
into plum blossoms

that barb the abandoned lot's
chain-link border.

2.

Weeds
a few feet thick

wind-combed
to a concave

where last week's rain
still evaporates.

3.

A silver
cellophane bag

floats there,
repels the sun

punctured past
overcast—

Boardwalk, Humboldt Bay

Pelican
slack then
stiff in free fall—

beak bent
toward the dredged
bay's surface.

Water brown
as the red-
wood trunks

stacked on
flatbed trucks
trudging down 101.

Greyhound, North Through Sonoma County

for Scott Pierce

1.

       Over the dusk-
tinted window
        vineyards flicker
and recede.

          Sun
blots out a mountain.

2.

Window
night makes

a mirror of—

my face
supplants
the landscape.

OUT OF LIGHT

...something of what we sense
may be true, may be the world, what it is, what we sense.

—William Bronk

To break

into the sight
of it—this
landscape—

how the light
makes do.
A thrust of

things—
a world—
words—

crush
against
the margin of you.

Weather

light-scripted
silence, a

hand's
shadow

writing
what

Switch

for Agnes Martin

Let the room
become
night, no light

to fracture its
forming form-
lessness—

a slow dissolve
of each
wall.

Seattle

hail re-
coils

from car
hood

half the
sky's

sun-
gashed

This

insists
winter's

bruise
in you;

a word,
love,

a wind.

Written

Light's token
to shadow
these winter-
stripped
limbs,
thawing,
shake over
the sidewalk's
pocked
inscriptions.

Without a Field Guide

Memory
skids across
daylight's
edges.

Moon
mistaken
for a
cloud.

Rewritten

Light
a spider scales
one branch
to the next
    tilts

in time
with the wind.
    Wind

revising
shadow
stretched

on a flat
patch of
tan grass.

After Frank Samperi

Wind begins
and with it
fog smudges
street-side shrubs,
weeds, lights, litter.

2:08 AM

versions
of silence

rain holds
close,

closing
around us

■

now
tree frogs

alliterate
the dark

February

rain's
remnants'

shape
splinters

window
night pulls

apart

Visible

for Rae Armantrout

Rain puddle's oil
streaks encircle
full moon   in pieces.

■

Frog chants percolate
through traffic static.

Full moon split by a pine branch.

■

Grease-splotched
parking lot a-
wash with dawn.

■

Leaves scrape a-
cross the road's

yellow
(worn-white)
        lines.

        ■

Light's wind's rhythm raked
        through these weeds poked

above a cinder block
        blotted in bird shit.

        ■

Wind's form fleshed
in this web's
gesture
                    outside
the closed window.

■

Fog clots
the window.

Hill   out
to the edge
                    visible.

Poem

Music this
distance
thins.

A throb
the horizon
swallows.

April

Through the
window, a-
cross

the floor,
bud-
blistered

limbs
broadcast
the hours.

Scale

Awakened
by the ticking,

not the alarm.

■

Gust of litter—now
the light's

obvious.

■

Gulls'

collapsed
song

weighs
sun.

Path

Weeds
whacked to pulp
between slits
in cinder
blocks laid
in gravel.
A path
to these
porch steps,
their chipped
blue paint
—the rain-
stained wood
cracked through.

Samoa Peninsula Jetty

Dead barnacles and gull shit grip the driftwood.

Your voice ahead of me. I stop to watch

the surf's thrown foam spot the rocks.

A buoy clangs against the downswell.

Arcata Marsh

Mudscape—tide's out—
out as far as fog gives sight.

Periphery-flecked,
orange-white
lichen latched to limbs

I thought were your
fingers—
your face turned
back by wind.

Patrick's Point

These waves, these
       light-patterns
the rock-clustered
           shore shatters

      find form again
          across our skin.

Stone Lagoon

Loops of bull kelp
smothered in

sea foam.
What you said

lodges under

a wave / disintegrates.

Ledge

By a stalk of
bramble thrust

up from brush
that skirts this

cliff ledge—
a humming-

bird hovers
thorn-level.

Shay Park

creek bed's
collected
reeds

exchange
shape
with

light

with

water

∎

upturned
trunk's
roots

caulked
by moss,
mud, what

sun

a web

snags

mud-
blackened

creek bank's
drainage

pipe's
rolled

r's

■

stone wall
a few ferns
fallen   there
            in place

tree's
red
bark

sounds
out

through
gnashed
brush

■

no more than
water

articulates
light

under the
bridge

ON A FALSE SPRING

This day writhes with what?

—Wallace Stevens

Page

We dredge
the silence

here, until
the nothing's

no longer
bare, barbed

by words
that won't say

what we cannot,
not knowing

how, why
they're there

pushing us
toward them.

Minor Alley

In day's diffusion
an afterthought
thaws.

I drink to this
abiding emptiness.

On the corner
a neon palm tree

stammers
through fog.

Clyfford Still

A dream's
white field

bursts into
morning.

I'm burned
awake here

where you
kept your eyes.

Brim with me
until empty,

and the wall
is the only

landscape
to walk

ourselves
wordless.

Another Room

Today
even the sun
is nothing to believe.

Windows
that won't open
for what winter remains.

On a False Spring

The names
we don't
remember, how

they flower—
smeared a-
long the field's

edge—
beyond our
mouths.

Drawn Out

Indoors for
days, I'm gone
in the sweep
of what
the window
gathers: sun-
set's heft serrated
between jagged
limbs hung limp
over the shed
roof's orange
rust, coils of under-
brush, the gaps
darkness articulates.

Within Weather

for Claire Donato

A rift in the cloud
as it carves
the hill's ridge, this sliced

light's slicing, blinds us.
Our words warped
to contain it—an

ache you could call song.

Hear

The field
throbs. Early
spring splits
a few things

open; I know
them, not
knowing their
names

—my only
company.
Here at the
margins

it's all said
illegibly.

Near

The hour when
all's gone
to rust,

red, shadow
in pursuit
of shadow

until every-
thing is
only that:

these various
registers of
black—

the unseen
seeing us
through.

Enough

Night rakes the landscape,
empties the room.
To speak

without speaking
through a gradual lack
of light—

a certain silence
rain dims to breath.

Plein Air

As if ink could speak
like this blind spot
interrupted by a breeze
seized in seizures of color.

Is there anything here
to say we're anywhere
at all? Blink and

focus on the cracked
concrete wall
left over
after the demolition

of a scorched Victorian
mansion. Follow
the phrasing of the

picket fence
bent back
in foliage
rich with thorns.

Morning Catalog

That sound's
the ocean's

collision
with traffic

ground down
to a thin hiss.

Day gathers
white—

too fucking white—
between buildings.

Rectangles
of shadow

on rectangles
of grass.

Where It Breaks

A voice unties
into mist
at sunset—
a voice
barely
absorbed
by silence.

The ocean's form
churns toward
stacked boulders
where it breaks
before breaking
again against
sand. Foam

enfolds
debris over-
flowing each
depression.

Photograph of a Mine

Somehow
the ground's

as hollow
as the sky.

■

Sheared
cliff face,
strewn
rock pile,

this heave
of machinery

—a stilted
vacancy.

■

Toward
a torn
cloud's
border

exhaust
plumes

pull

a-

part.

Poem Including History

A curb the color
of nausea.
Parking lot gravel

splintered with glass,
dog shit, receipts.
Storage sheds—a row

of lamp-lit doors
deepening
as dusk thickens. Now,

night, they're all that's left
and traffic's
excuse for music

moving through the room.

Drunken Spring

for Tony Robinson

April's protrusions
puncture my
vision, my resolve

not to remember
through that which
floods us forgetful.

One season to the
next, and still
the same light lingers.

At Once

for Chris Rizzo

A thought collapses
beneath the weight of

bird noise needling
the bedroom walls.

All of this green
breathing shadow

breathes spring
all at once. I

enter a trance
tracing each trace.

Words, where
my mind nests,

return me to heart.

And All Around

Branches sift
the sky's
blot, thread

the moon
thin.
Dawn

drawn
into and
out of itself.

Last Spring

On the horizon
what you thought
was exhaust
from the pulp mill
was rain frayed
over the mountains—
mottled blue,
black—caught
in the foreground
locked by eucalyptus.

ACKNOWLEDGMENTS:

Many of these poems previously appeared in chapbooks: *Within Hours* (The Fault Line Press), *Bramble* (Hot Whiskey Press), *Property Line* (Fewer & Further Press), *November Graph* (Longhouse), and *Out of Light* (Kitchen Press).

And some of these poems, quite often in different versions, have appeared in journals and magazines: *2River, Ah Bartleby!, American Poet: The Journal of the Academy of American Poets, Asterisk, BafterC, Barrelhouse, Bimbo Gun, Bongos of the Lord, Cannibal, Carve, Cranky, The Cultural Society, Effing Magazine, Eucalyptus, Hassle, Kadar Koli, Knockout, LIT, La Fovea, Mirage/(Period)ical, Mrs. Maybe, NOÖ Journal, The Nation, Noon, The Northwest Review, Origin, Small Town, Teeny Tiny, Tight, The Tiny,* and *Wildlife.*

A small handful of poems from *Bramble* and *Property Line* appeared in the anthology *For the Time Being: The Bootstrap Book of Poetic Journals,* edited by Tyler Doherty and Tom Morgan.

My gratitude to the editors.

Thank you: Shannon Tharp, Jess Mynes, Andrew Mister, Anthony Robinson, Jack Hirschman, James Ginn, Fran Ryan, Frank Sherlock, Kyle Conner, C.A. Conrad, Thomas Devaney, Dr. Robynne Lute, Zach Barocas, Pam Rehm, Christopher Rizzo, Aaron Tieger, Scott Pierce, Ryan Murphy, Claire Donato, Justin Marks, Melissa Hammesfahr, Andrew Hughes, Caleb Nichols, John Phillips, Steven Moore, Mike Young, Floyd Yowell, and Humboldt County, California—for the company.

Joseph Massey was born in 1978 in Chester, Pennsylvania, and has spent the last seven years in Humboldt County, California, where all of the poems in this book—his first full-length collection—were written.

CPSIA information can be obtained at www.ICGtesting.com
Printed in the USA
LVOW06s0021190714

395013LV00001B/32/P